OLD SCOTS PROVERBS

£4.95

INTRODUCTION

Gie your tongue mair holidays than your heid...Gie a beggar a bed, and he'll pay you wi' a louse...The lass that has mony wooers aften wails the warst...Better half hangit than ill married...He needs a lang shanket spoon that sups kail wi' the Deil!

All the above proverbs sum up the straight talking attitude that has been a trait of the Scots character for generations.

In "The Old Scots Proverbs" we present a selection from the collected works of Andrew Henderson which was published at Glasgow in 1881 by Thomas D. Morison.

Dozens of topics are covered in an easy to follow A-Z format. These include beauty, courage, courtship, death, destiny, dress, drunkenness, folly, fortune, friendship, greed, health, happiness, laughter, marriage, poverty, pride etc. etc.

Much sound advice is offered. Those who work in pubs are warned that "ale-sellers should not be tale-tellers." Nosey-parkers are advised "Listen at a keyhole and ye'll hear news o' yoursel?" On the subject of living beyond our means we are told that "a poor man's debt makes muckle noise!" Those who take out hire purchase are informed that "they who hae maist need o' credit seldom get muckle."

A neat proverb to sum up good triumphing over evil is the one that reads:- "The deil goes awa' when he finds the door steeket against him." Lazy folk are told that "an idle brain is the deil's smiddy." On a similar theme: "If the deil finds an idle man he sets him to wark."

On a lighter note our cover illustration sums up how some money can help ease life's problems—"a penny in the purse is a merry companion." The back cover illustrates that "the lass who has many wooers aften wails the warst." These and all the other illustrations are by John Mackay.

Published by Lang Syne Publishers Ltd
45 Finnieston St., Glasgow
Tel: 041-204 3104
Printed by Dave Barr Print
45 Finnieston Street, Glasgow
Tel: 041-221 2598

AGE.

An auld man's a bedfu' o' banes.
Auld age and marriage bring a man to his night-cap.
Auld folk are twice bairns.
Haud your feet, Lucky Dad, auld fouk's no fiery.
[Mind your feet, grandfather, old people are not nimble.]
He's auld and cauld, and ill to lie aside.
There's beild beneath an auld man's beard.

ANGER.

Anger begins wi' folly, and ends wi' repentance.
Anger canna stand without a strong hand.
Anger is the fever and frenzy of the soul.
Anger's mair hurtfu' than the wrang that caused it.
Anger's short lived in a gude man.
Anger maks a rich man hated, and a poor man scorned.
Anger may glance into the breast o' a wise man, but only rests
     i' the bosom o' a fool.
Anger punishes itsel'.
He's ne'er at ease that's angry.
He that's angry opens his mouth and steeks his een.
[The angry man speaks unadvisedly, without investigating the matter.]
He that will be angry for ony thing, will be angry for naething.
Twa things ne'er be angry wi',—what ye can help, and what ye
     canna help.

AVARICE.

Avarice generally miscalculates, and as generally deceives.
He wad fley a louse for its skin.
Mony ane for land, taks a fool by the hand.
[Many marry for money.]
Ne'er let your gear ourgang you.
[Pride not yourself in your riches.]

BAIRNS.

Bairns are certain care but nae sma' joy.
Bairns maun creep ere they gang.
[Those who don't succeed very well at first may do better afterwards.]
Bairns speak in the field what they hear by the fireside.

Between three and thirteen, thraw the woodie when it's green.

[Youth is the time for training.]

Gie a bairn his will and a whelp its fill, and neither will do weel.

He's a wise bairn that kens his ain father.

Ill bairns are best heard at hame.

Of bairns' gifts ne'er be fain: nae sooner they gie then they seek it again.

Put anither man's bairn in your bosom, and he'll creep out at your sleeve.

[Though you cherish another man's child, he will have no natural affection towards you.]

Silly bairns are eith o' lear.

We can shape our bairns' wyliecoat, but canna shape their weird.

[We can shape our children's clothes, but not their fate.]

When bairns are young they gar their parents' heads ache; when they are auld they mak their hearts ache.

BEAUTY.

A bonnie bride's soon buskit.

[For her beauty requires little adornment.)

A bonnie face needs nae band, an ill ane deserves nane.

[*Band*, a ribbon.]

A fair face and a foul bargain.

A fair face is half a fortune.

Beauty but bounty availeth nothing.

[Beauty without goodness is of little worth.]

Beauty's a fair but a fading flower.

Beauty's muck when honour's tint.

[Beauty is of no value when honour is lost.]

Beauty without virtue's like poison in a gowd box.

BEGGARY.

Beggars breed, and rich men feed.

Beggars shouldna be choosers.

Beg frae beggars, ye'll ne'er be rich.

Gie a beggar a bed, and he'll pay you wi' a louse.
Set a beggar on horseback, and he'll ride to the deil.

BLINDNESS.

A blind man has nae need o' a looking-glass.
A blind man's wife needs nae painting.
A nod's as gude as a wink to a blind horse.
He's blind that eats marrow, but far blinder that lets him.
The blind mare is first in the mire.

BOASTING.

A' the corn's no shorn by kempers.
  [All the work is not done by those who excel at it.]
A man may spit in his loof and do but little.
  [May make a show of working.]
A vaunter and a liar are muckle about ae thing.
  [Are much the same.]

BREEDING.

A weel bred dog gaers out when he sees them preparing to kick
  him out.
Birth's gude but breeding's better.
Dogs bark as they are bred.
Gude breeding and siller mak our sons gentlemen.

BUTTER.

Butter and burn trouts are kittle meat for maidens.
Butter is gowd i' the morning, siller at noon, and copper at night.
Butter to butter 's nae kitchen.
Fry stanes wi' butter and the broo will be gude.
He that has routh o' butter may lay it the thicker on his bread.

CARE.

A pund o' care winna pay an ounce o' debt.
  ['Care' here means 'trouble of mind.']
Care will kill a cat, and she has nine lives.
Little gear, less care.

Gie a beggar a bed, and he'll pay you wi a louse.

CAUSE AND EFFECT.

A crooked stick will throw a crooked shadow.
A green Yule maks a fat kirk-yard.
A gude hairst maks men prodigal, and a bad ane provident.
A light-heeled mither maks a leaden-heeled dochter.
A rowing stane gathers nae fog.
As the sow fills the draff sours.
 [As the stomach fills food loses its relish.]
Nae whip cuts sae sharp as the lash o' conscience.

CAUTION.

Better greet ower your gudes than after your gudes.
Canny stretch, soon reach.
Cawk is nae shears.
 [From the tailor's marking out his cloth with chalk before he cuts it.
  It does not follow that a plan laid out will be executed.]
Haud the hank in your ain hand.
He needs a lang shanket spoon that sups kail wi' the deil.
 [Those that have to do with wicked men require to be on their guard.]
He that has but ae ee, maun tent it weel.
If you dinna see the bottom, dinna wade.
 [Don't venture upon an undertaking which you can't see your way
  through.]
Ne'er misca' a Gordon in the raws o' Strathbogie.
 [Strathbogie was the district of the Gordons. Never speak ill of a man on
  his own ground.]
Ne'er put your hand farer out than your sleeve will reach.
 [Spend no more than you can afford.]
Ne'er say 'ill fallow' to him you deal wi'.
 ['Ill fallow' bad fellow.]
Ne'er trust muckle to an auld enemy, nor a new friend.
Silence and thoughts hurt nae man.

CHARITY.

Charity begins at hame, but shouldna end there.
Charity ne'er made a man poor, nor robbery rich, nor prosperity
 wise.
Giving to the poor increaseth a man's store.
Spend, and God will send; spare, and be bare.

He needs a lang shanket spoon that sups kail wi' the deil.

CONTENTMENT.

A man's weel or wae, as he thinks himsel sae.
A man's greatest wealth is contentment wi' little.
Ane at a time is gude fishing.
Contentment is a constant feast.
Hap and a ha'penny, is world's gear aneugh.
O' a little tak a little, and leave a little behin.
O' a little tak a little; when there's nought, tak a'.

COURAGE.

A courageous foe is better than a cowardly friend.
A faint heart never won a fair lady.
A man's aye crouse in his ain cause.
Courage against misfortune, and reason against passion.
Fortune favours the brave.
Fortune helps the hardy, and the poltroon aye repels.
Naething sae bauld as a blind mare.

COURTSHIP.

A flyer wad aye hae a follower.
> [Said of a girl running from a young man on purpose that he should follow her.]

Glowering is nae gainsaying.
Happy is the wooing that's no lang o' doing.
He that woos a maiden maun come seldom in her sight;
—He that woos a widow maun ply her day and night.
Light maidens mak langing lads.
Nipping and scarting is Scotch folks' wooing.
Sunday's wooing draws to ruin.
The lass that has mony wooers aften wails the warst.
Wha may woo without cost?
When petticoats woo, breeks may come speed.
> [Said when maids court young men.]

COWARDICE.

A coward's nae company.
A coward's fear maks a coward brave.
A man may spit in his nieve and do but little.
A wee thing fleys a coward.

The lass that has mony wooers aften wails the warst.

CREDIT.

Credit is better than ill won gear.
Credit keeps the crown o' the causey.
Credit lost is like a broken glass.
He wha's lost his credit is dead to the warld.
They that hae maist need o' credit seldom get muckle.

CUNNING.

A crafty man's ne'er at peace.
Craft maun hae claes, but truth gaes naked.
He can say, My jo, and think it no.
　　[He can pretend to be kind without being so.]
He's no sae daft as he lets on.
He kens how mony beans mak five.
　　[He can look after his own interests.]
He kens how to butter a whitten.
He kens which side his bannock's buttered on.
　　[The three preceding have the same meaning.]
He snoits his nose in his neighbour's cog, to get the brose himsel.
His e'ening sang and his morning sang are no baith alike.
The peasweep aye cries farest frae its ain nest.
They that see your head see not a' your height.
　　[Said to men of low stature and high spirits.]

DEATH.

A dry cough is the trumpeter o' death.
Death and marriage break term-days.
Death comes in and speirs nae questions.
Death defies the doctor.
Death is deaf, and will hear nae denial.
He wha's poor when he's married, shall be rich when he's
　　buried.
The death o' ae bairn winna skail a house.
There's remede for a' thing, but stark dead.

DEBT.

A poor man's debt maks muckle noise.
A pound o' care winna pay an ounce o' debt.
Better auld debts than auld sairs.
　　[The debts may come in, but the sores will ache.]
He wha pays his debt begins to make a stock.

Out o' debt, out o' danger.
Sins and debts are aye mair than we think them.
The less debt the mae dainties.

DELAY.

Delays are dangerous.
Delay not till to-morrow what may be done to-day.
There's naething got by delay, but dirt and lang nails.

DESTINY.

A man may woo wha he will, but must wed whare he's weird.
Flee as fast as you will, your fortune will be at your tail.
Hanging gaes by hap.
He that's born to be hanged will never be drowned.
It was my luck, my lady, and I canna get by it.
Nae butter will stick to my bread.
[No good fortune comes my way.]
Nae fleeing frae fate.
Some hae hap, and some stick in the gap.
The water will ne'er waur the widdie.
[The water will never cheat the gallows.]

DEVIL.

If that God give, the deil daurna reave.
I like him as the deil likes holy water.
It's curly and crookit, as the deil said o' his horns.
Speak o' ony body but the deil and he'll appear.
Speak o' the deil and he'll appear.
[Said when the person we have been speaking of happens to come in.]
The deil and the dean begin wi' ae letter:
—When the deil gets the dean, the kirk will be the better.
The deil aye drives his hogs to an ill market.
The deil bides his day.

The deil gaes awa when he finds the door steeket against him.
The deil's a busy bishop in his ain diocese.
The deil's aye gude to his ain.
The deil's bairns hae aye their daddy's luck.

[Said maliciously when we observe the prosperity of those we esteem not.]

The deil's cow calves twice a year.
The devil was sick, and the devil a monk would be;
—The devil got well, and the devil a monk was he.

[Those who make good resolutions in time of trouble often forget them in
prosperity.]

DIFFIDENCE.

A blate cat maks a proud mouse.

[Lax discipline is apt to be taken advantage of.]

Diffidence is the mother o' safety.
He that spares to speak, spares to speed.

[He that hesitates to speak on his own behalf when occasion offers will not
readily improve his position.]

Mony an honest man needs help, that hasna the face to seek it.

DIRT.

Cleanliness is nae pride, dirt is nae honesty.
Dirt bodes luck.
Dirt defies the king.
Dirt parts gude companie.

[Said when unwelcome persons join a company.]

He's a dirty tod that fyles his ain hole.
He that deals in dirt has aye foul fingers.
'Lang straes are nae motes,' quo' the wife, when she hauled the
    cat out o' the kirn.
The clartier the cosier.
The fish that's bred in a dirty puddle will aye taste o' mud.
The mair dirt, the less hurt.

DRESS.

Bonnie feathers mak bonnie birds.
Gude claes open a' doors.
You're as braw as Binks' wife, when she becket to the minister,
    wi' the dish-clout on her head.

The deil gaes awa when he finds the door steeket against him.

DRUNKENNESS.

A red nose maks a ragged back.
Double drinks are gude for drouth.
Drink and drouth come seindle thegither.
Drink little, that ye may drink lang.
Drunk at night and dry next morning.
Drunk folk seldom take harm.
Fair fa' gude drink, for it gars folk speak as they think.
He's waur to water than to corn.
  [Fonder of drink than of his food.]
He speaks in his drink what he thinks in his drouth.
Laith to drink, and laith frae it.
  [Unwilling and slow to begin, but once begun, equally so to leave off.]
Ne'er let the nose blush for the sins o' the mouth.
    Our fathers, who were wondrous wise,
    —Did wash their throats before they washed their eyes.
Tak a hair o' the dog that bit you yestreen.
  [One suffering from the effect of the previous night's drinking is
  recommended to take a little more to cure him.]
The maut's aboon the meal.
  [There's more drink than food.]
What soberness conceals, drunkenness reveals.
What you do when you're drunk, you must pay for when you're
    sober.
When drink's in, wit's out.

EARLY RISING.

Early birds catch the worms.
He that wad thrive, must rise by five;
—He that has thriven, may lie till seven.
They that rise with the sun, hae their work weel begun.
They wha are early up and hae nae business, hae either an ill
    bed, an ill wife, or an ill conscience.

EATING.

Eat in measure, and defy the doctor.
Eating needs but a beginning.
Eating and cleaning only require a beginning.
Eating and drinking puts awa the stamach.
Eat peas wi' a prince, and cherries wi' a chapman.
  ["Peas are best when young, and cherries when ripe."—*Kelly's Scottish
  Proverbs.*]
Live not to eat, but eat to live.

Tak a hair o' the dog that bit you yestreen.

ECONOMY.

A penny hained's a penny gained.

A penny hained's a penny clear, and a preen a-day's a groat a-year.

Better lang little, than soon naething.

E'ening orts are gude morning's fother.

[What is despised to-day may be valued to-morrow.]

Frae saving comes having.

He that hains his dinner wil hae the mair to his supper.

If he binds the pock, she'll sit doon on 't.

[Said when a niggardly man is married to a more niggardly wife.]

Keep a thing seven years, and you'll find a use for it.

Ken when to spend, and when to spare, and when to buy, and you'll ne'er be bare.

Lay your wame to your winning.

[Let not your household expenditure exceed your income.]

Want not, waste not.

Wha winna keep a penny will never hae any.

Wide will wear, but tight will tear.

ENVY.

Envy is cured by true friendship, as coquetry is by true love.

Envy is the rack of the soul, and torture of the body.

Envy ne'er does a gude turn, but when it means an ill ane.

EVIL.

Of ae' ill come mony.

Of ill debtors men get aiths.

Of twa ills choose the least.

EVIL COMPANY.

Gude company on a journey is worth a coach.

He keeps his road weel eneugh, wha gets rid o' ill company.

Ill council will gar a man stick his ain mare.

Keep out o' his company, wha cracks o' his cheatery.

[Who talks of his cheating or cunning.]

Tell me the company you keep, and I'll tell you your character.

EVIL CONDUCT.

A libertine life is not a life of liberty.
Do weel and hae weel.
>He that hath and winna keep it;
>He that wants and winna seek it;
>He that drinks and is not dry;
>Siller shall want as weel as I.

He that ill does, never gude weens.
>[Never thinks any good of others.]

Your conduct will gar you claw a beggar's haffet yet.
>[Will reduce you to beggary.]

EVIL DISPOSITION.

An ill-willie cow should hae short horns.
>[Ill natured people should not have much authority, for they are sure to
>abuse it.]

Buy a thief frae the widdie, and he'll cut your throat.
He that does you an ill turn will ne'er forgie you.
Say what you will, an ill mind will turn 't to ill.
The toolyeing tyke comes limping hame.
Ye're like the witches, ye can do nae gude to yoursel.

EVIL EXAMPLE.

If ae sheep loup ower the dike, a' the lave will follow.
If the laird slight the lady, sae will the kitchen boy.
If a mare hae a bald face, the filly will hae a blaze.
If you gang a year wi' a cripple, you'll limp at the end o 't.

EVIL SPEAKING.

A gossip speaks ill o' a', and a' o' her.
Gie your tongue mair holidays than your head.
He that has gall in his mouth canna spit honey.
He that speaks what he should not will hear what he would not.
Ill never speaks well.
It's a gude tongue that says nae ill, but a better heart that thinks
nane.
Ne'er speak ill o' the dead.
Ne'er speak ill o' them whase bread ye eat.
Sometimes words cut mair than swords.

A gossip speaks ill o' a' and o' o' her.

EXAMPLE.

As the auld cock craws, the young cock learns.
Every act is best taught by example.
Example goes before precept.

EXPERIENCE.

A man at forty is either a fool or a physician.
An auld mason maks a gude barrowman.
Burnt bairns dread the fire.
Experience is gude, but aften dear bought.
Experience is the mither o' invention.
Experience is the mither of tool-grinding.
Experience teaches fools, and fools will learn nae ither way.
If things were to be done twice, ilka ane wad be wise.

EXTREMES.

A' owers are ill, but ower the water and ower the hill.
Langest at the fireside soonest finds cauld.
Like the dam o' Devon, lang gathered and soon gane.
Mair than aneugh is ower muckle.
Ower muckle o' ae thing is gude for naething.
Ye're either a' dirt or a' butter.
    [Equally extreme in fondness and aversion.]

FEAR.

He's mair fleyed than hurt.
There's nae medicine for fear.
You're feared for the day you never saw.

FLATTERY.

A flatterer is a dangerous enemy.
Of a' flatterers, self-love is the greatest.
Plaster thick and some will stick.
When flatterers meet, the deil gaes to his dinner.

FOLLY.

A fool and his money are soon parted.

A fool is mair happy in thinking weel o' himsel, than a wise man is of ithers thinking weel o' him.

A fool may earn money, but it taks a wise man to keep it.

A fool may find faults that a wise man canna mend.

A fool may gie a wise man an advice.

A fool may speir mae questions than a wise man can answer.

A fool's bolt is soon shot.

A' fails that fools think.

A man at five may be a fool at fifteen.

A man may speak like a wise man, and act like a fool.

A nod frae a lord is a breakfast for a fool.

A rogue detected is the greatest fool.

Change o' weather finds discourse for fools.

Dogs and bairns are aye fond o' fools.

Fools and bairns shouldna see half done wark.

Fools mak feasts, and wise men eat them;
Wise men mak jests, and fools repeat them.

Fools bigg houses, and wise men buy them.

Fools laugh at their ain sport.

He has some sma' wit, but a fool has the guiding o't.

He's a fool that asks ower muckle, but he's a greater fool that gies it.

He's no the fool that the fool is, but he that wi' the fool deals.

He that clatters till himsel cracks to a fool.

He that taks his gear and gies it to his bairns,
—Were weel saired to take a mell and ding out his harns.

[
"Taken from the history of one John Bell, who having given his whole substance to his children, was by them neglected; after he died there was found in his chest a mallet with this inscription—

I John Bell leaves here a mell,

The man to fell, who gives all

To his bairns, and keep nothing

To himsell."—*Kelly's Scottish Proverbs.*]

It's folly to live poor and die rich.

Nae fools like auld fools.

Twa fools in ae house is a couple ower mony.

FORESIGHT.

A steek in time saves nine.

> Canny chiels carry cloaks when it's fair,
> The fool, when it's foul, has nane to wear.

Gude foresight furthers the wark.

FORTUNE.

A lucky man needs little counsel.

An inch o' gude luck is worth a fathom o' forecast.

Better be the lucky man than the lucky man's son.

Flee you ne'er sae fast, your fortune will be at your tail.

Put your hand in the creel, tak out an adder or an eel.
> [Said of taking a wife.]

There's nae fence against ill fortune.

Twa heads may lie on ae cod, and nane ken whare the luck lies.
> ["Spoken when either husband or the wife is dead, and the surviving party
> goes back in the world after."—*Kelly's Scottish Proverbs*.]

FRIENDSHIP.

A faithful friend is the medicine of life.

A father is a treasure, a brither is a comfort, but a friend is baith.

A friend at court is worth a penny in the purse.

A friend in need is a friend indeed.

A friend's dinner is soon dicht.
> [Because he will be easily contented.]

A friend's ne'er kenned till he's needed.

A friend to a', is a friend to nane.

A gude friend is ne'er tint, but an ill ane's at hand

Be slow in choosing a friend, but slower in changing him.

Buy friendship wi' presents and it will be bought frae you.

Change your friend ere you hae need.

Choose your friend amang the wise, and your wife amang the
  virtuous.

Friends are like fiddle-strings, they maunna be screwed ower
  tight.

Friends gree best at a distance.

Friendship is stronger than kindred.

Friendship multiplies our joy, and divides our grief.

Hearts may agree, though heads differ.

It's no tint that a friend gets.

Life without a friend is death with a witness.

My son is my son until he gets a wife,
My dochter is my dochter a' the days o' her life.
Nae man can be happy without a friend,—nor be sure of him
until he's unhappy.
Quhen welth aboundis, mony friends we number:
Quhen guidis dekay, then friends flie away.
Suffering for a friend doubleth friendship.
Try your friend before you hae need o' him.

GENTILITY.

A gentleman should hae mair in his pouch than on his back.
A gentleman without an estate is like a pudding without suet.
Gentility without ability is waur than plain beggary.
Gentle puddocks hae lang taes.
   [Those in authority and power can reach you though at a distance;
      Therefore provoke them not.]
Gentry sent to the market winna buy a peck o' meal.

GIFT.

A gien horse shoudna be looked i' the mouth.
A gift wi' a kind look is a double present.
He doubles his gift that gies 't in time.
Muckle gifts mak beggars bauld.
Naething is freer than a gift.
The wife's aye welcome that comes wi' a crooket oxter.
   [That comes with a present, the arm being bent in carrying it.]
They that come wi' a gift dinna need to stand lang at the door.

GLUTTONY.

A cram'd kyte maks a crazy carcase.
A man may dig his grave wi' his teeth.
Muckle meat, mony maladies.
Mutton is sweet, and gars mony die ere they be sick.
   [Makes people steal sheep for which they get hanged.]
Suppers kill mair than doctors cure.

GOD.

Forsake not God till you find a better master.

Gie God the first and the last of every day.

Gie your heart to God, and your awms to the poor.

God is kind to fou folk and bairns.

> [From the remarkable manner in which young children and drunken people escape injury.]

God sends water to the well that folk thinks will ne'er be dry.

> ["Spoken when our poor kin and followers are always asking of us; as if we should never be exhausted."—*Kelly.*]

God sends fools fortunes.

God sends us claith according to our cauld.

God shapes the back for the burden.

God tempers the wind to the new shorn lamb.

GOOD.

A gude cause maks a stout heart and a strong arm.

A gude conscience is the best divinity.

A gude example is the best sermon.

A gude life is the only religion.

A gude life maks a happy death.

A gude name is better than a fou house.

A gude paymaster never wants hands to work.

GOOD CONDUCT.

Adversity overcome is the greatest glory.

Do the likeliest and hope the best.

Do weel and doubt nae man, do ill and doubt a' men.

Do weel and dread nae shame.

Do what you ought and let come what will.

Keep gude company and ye'll be counted ane o' them.

Send your son to Ayr: if he did weel here he'll do weel there.

Tell the truth and shame the deil.

There is more glory in forgiving an injury, than there is pleasure in revenging it.

GRATITUDE.

A borrowed lend should gae laughing hame.

> [A loan should be returned with thanks and grace.]

Ae gude turn deserves anither.

Gratitude is a heavy burden.

Gratitude preserves auld friendships and begets new.

Gudewill ne'er wants time to show itsel.

Gudewill should aye be taen in part o' payment.

A man may dig his grave wi' his teeth.

GREED.

A greedy ee ne'er gat a fou wame.
>[Greedy persons are never satisfied.]

A greedy ee ne'er gat a gude pennyworth.

A greedy guts ne'er got a gude meltith.

Greedy fouk hae lang arms.

He can hide his meat and seek mair.
>["Spoken when covetous people pretend poverty; and conceal their wealth to plead pity."—*Kelly.*]

He's like a bagpipe, he's ne'er heard till his wame's fou.

He looks as he would swallow it.

He that has muckle would aye hae mair.

He'll hae aneugh some day, when his mouth's fou o' mools.
>[He'll have enough when his mouth is filled with the earth of the grave.]

He'll no gie the head for the washing.
>[He'll not readily part with his own interest.]

Ye ne'er see green cheese but your een reels.

Ye wad marry a midden for the muck.

HABIT.

Ae year a nurse, and seven years a daw.
>[Because in that year she will contract a habit of idleness.]

An ill custom is like a gude cake—better broken than kept.

Auld sparrows are ill to tame.

Ca' a cow to the ha', and she'll rin to the byre.

HAPPINESS.

A blythe heart makes a blooming look.

A wee housie weel filled; a wee piece land weel tilled; a wee wifie weel willed,—will make a happy man.

Every inch of joy has an ell of annoy.

He's no the happiest man that has the maist gear.

It's no what we hae, but what we do wi' what we hae, that maks us happy or miserable.

HASTE.

Bargains made in a hurry are aften repented o' at leisure.
Haste and anger hinder gude counsel.
Haste maks waste, and waste maks want, and want maks strife
    between the gudeman and gudewife.
Hasty was hanged, but Speed-o'-foot wan awa.
    [*Wan awa,* succeeded in getting away.]
sThere's a het hurry when there's a hen to roost.

HEALTH.

Ae hour's cauld will sook out seven years' heat.
After dinner sit a while; after supper walk a mile.
A gude wife and health is a man's best wealth.
Be lang sick, that ye may be soon weel.
Better wait on the cook than on the doctor.
Broken bread maks hale bairns.
Cast not a clout till May be out.
Gude health is better than wealth.
He what eats but ae dish seldom needs the doctor.
Health is the best wealth.
If you wish to be healthy, clothe warmly and eat sparingly.
Light suppers mak lang life.
Raw dauds mak fat lads.
The town for wealth, the country for health.

HELP.

God helps them that help themselves.
Help is gude at a' thing, except at the cog.
    [Except when taking food.]

HOME.

East or west, hame is best.
Hame is hame, be't ever sae hamely.
There's nae place like hame, quo' the deil, when he fand himsel
    i' the Court o' Session.

HONESTY.

Honesty may be dear bought, but can ne'er be an ill pennyworth.
Mony an honest man needs help that hasna the face to seek it.
Naething is a man's truly but what he cometh by duly.
O' a' crafts to be an honest man is the master-craft.
Open confession is gude for the saul.
The nod o' an honest man is aneugh.

HOPE.

He wha lives on hope has a slender diet.
He wha lives on hope will die fasting.
If it werena for hope, the heart would break.
Nane are sae weel but they hope to be better.
When the heart's past hope, the face is past shame.

HUMAN LIFE.

A reeky house and a scolding wife.
Will lead a man a fashious life.
A winter day, and a wintry way, is the life o' man.
Be thou weel, or be thou wae, you will not be aye sae.
God's providence has balanced peculiar sufferings with peculiar
    enjoyments.
Life consists not in breathing but in enjoying life.
Trouble and adversity mak greatness and prosperity far mair
    pleasant.
When hope and hap, (when health and wealth) are highest,
—Then woe and wreck, (disease and death) are nighest.

HUNGER.

A hungry louse bites sair.
A hungry man is an angry man.
Hunger me and I'll harry thee.
    [Servants badly fed are apt to steal.]
Hunger never fails of a gude cook.
Hunger will break through stane wa's.
Hungry dogs are blythe o' bursten puddins.
Hungry dogs will eat dirty puddins.

IDLENESS.

An idle brain is the deil's smiddy.
An idle man is the deil's bolster.
By doing naething we learn to do ill.
Idle dogs worry sheep.
Idle young, needy auld.
If the deil finds an idle man he sets him to wark.
He's idle, that might be better employed.
He that gapes till he be fed, will gape till he be dead.
Naething is got without pains but dirt and lang nails.

INDUSTRY.

A gude beginning maks a gude ending.
A gude day's darg may be done wi' a dirty spade.
Ae hour in the morning is worth twa at night.
Ay wark and nae ploy, maks Jock a dull boy.
Nae gains without pains.
Nae sweat, nae sweet.
Naething is got without pains but an ill name.
Naething is sae difficult but may be overcome wi' perseverance.
Perseverance performs greater works than strength.
Plough deep while sluggards sleep.
    The fit (foot) on the cradle, the hand on the reel,
    Is the sign o' a woman that means to do weel.

JEALOUSY.

As ye do yoursel, ye judge o' your neighbour.
If the auld wife hadna been in the oven hersel, she ne'er wad hae
    thought o' looking for her dochter there.
Twa o' ae trade seldom agree.
    Twa cats and ae mouse—twa mice in ae house—
    Twa dogs and ae bane—ne'er will agree in ane.

JESTING.

Bitter jests poison friendship.
He that maks folk afraid o' his wit, should be afraid o' their
    memories.
Leave a jest when it pleases you best.
Mony a true tale's tauld in jest.

JUSTICE.

A gude cause makes a strong arm.
Do as ye wad be done to.
Live and let live.
The sin is no in taking a gude price but in giein' ill measure.
When ilka ane gets his ain, the thief will get the widdie.

KINDNESS.

A kindly word cools anger.
A man may be kind, and gie little o' his gear.
Favours unused are favours abused.
Kindness is like cress seed—increases by sowing.

LAUGHTER.

As lang lives the merry man as the sad.
Laugh and grow fat.
Laugh at leisure, ye may greet ere e'en.
They showed their back teeth laughing.

LEARNING.

By learning naething we learn to do ill.
 Learn young, learn fair.
 Learn auld, learn mair.
Ne'er ower auld to learn.
We're aye to learn as lang as we live.

LOVE.

Cauld cools the love that kindles ower het.
Fanned fires and forced love ne'er did weel.
He that loves dearly chides severely.
Love is as warm amang cottars as courtiers.
Love is ne'er without jealousy.
Love is without law.
Love looks o'er mony faults.
Love thinks nae ill, envy speaks nae gude.
Nae herb will cure love.
Perfect love canna be without equality.

They showed their back teeth laughing.

LYING.

A liar is an economist of truth.

A liar should hae a gude memory.

He never lies but when the holland's green.

[That is always, for the holly is ever green.]

If a lie could hae worried you, you would hae been dead langsyne.

Poets and painters hae leave to lie.

MANNERS.

Meat feeds, claith cleads, but manners mak the man.

Meat is gude but mense is better.

Ye hae gude manners, but ye bear them not about wi' you.

MARRIAGE.

A man canna wive and thrive the same year.

Better half hanged than ill married.

Better marry ower the midden than ower the muir.

[Better marry among those you know than among strangers.]

He's a fool wha marries at Yule, for when the bairn's to bear the corn's to shear.

He that marries a widow will hae a dead man's head often thrown in his dish.

He that marries before he is wise will die before he thrive.

He wha marries for love without money hath merry nights and sorry days.

He wha tells his wife a' is but shortly married.

If gude marriages are made in heaven, whare are the bad anes made?

If marriages are made in heaven, you hae few friends there.

[Because you have a bad wife.]

Marriage and hanging gae by destiny.

Marriages and deaths break term days.

Married folks are like rats in a trap—fain to get ithers in, but fain to be out themsels.

Marry a beggar and get a louse for your tocher.

Marry aboon your match and get a master.

Marry for love and work for siller.

Marry your son when you will, but your dochter when you can.

Never marry a widow unless her first husband was hanged.

Wedding and ill wintering tame both man and beast.

Wha marries between the sickle and the scythe will never thrive.

Y hae tied a knot wi' your tongue you winna loose wi' your teeth.

He that marries a widow will have a dead man's head often thrown in his dish.

NECESSITY.

Ane may think that daurna speak.
Any port in a storm.
He'll rather turn than burn.
Necessity has nae law.
Necessity is a hard master.
Necessity's the mither o' invention.
Need maks greed.
Need maks the auld wife trot.

NEIGHBOURS.

A great man and a great river are often ill neighbours.
I would rather strive wi' the great rigg than wi' an ill neighbour.
   ["An apology of him that takes a larger farm than we suppose he can
   manage: That he would rather do his best with it than be vexed with the
   contentions of an ill partner."—*Kelly.*]
We can live without our friends, but no without our neighbour.

PATIENCE.

Dree out the inch as ye hae done the span.
   [Endure unto the end.]
He that canna thole maun flit man a hole.
Patience is a plaster for a' sairs.
Patience wi' poverty is a man's best remedy.
Thole weel is gude for burning.

PLENTY.

He kensna the pleasures o' plenty, wha ne'er felt the pains o'
   penury.
Plenty maks dainty.
Wealth gars wit waver.

POVERTY.

A light purse maks a heavy heart.

A poor man gets a poor marriage.

An empty purse fills the face wi' wrinkles.

As poor as a kirk mouse.

Aye taking out o' the meal pock and ne'er putting in't soon
comes to the bottom.

It's sin, and no poverty, that maks a man miserable.

Mony ane would hae been waur had their estates been better.

Pennyless sould maun pine in purgatory.

The back and the belly keep the hands busy.

When we want, friends are scant.

When poverty comes in at the door, love flees out by the
window.

Wi' an empty hand nae man can hawks lure.

[No one will serve you for nothing.]

PRIDE.

A proude heart in a poor breast has muckle dolour to dree.

A proud mind and a beggar's purse agree ill thegither.

A twalpenny cat may look at the king.

Alike ilka day maks a clout on Sunday.

[Don't wear your best clothes every day or they won't be fit for Sunday.]

A's no gowd that glitters.

An only dochter is either a deil or a daw.

Arrogance is a weed that grows maistly in a midden.

As gude may haud the stirrup as he that loups on.

As you thrive your feet fails you.

[The farther you go, the farther behind. Said when people meet with
unexpected interruptions in their business.]

He struts like a craw in a gutter.

He thinks himsel nae page's peer.

He thinks himsel worth muckle mice dirt.

I wish I had as muckle black pepper, as he thinks himsel worthy
o' mice dirt.

[Said of the self-conceited.]

Pride and grace ne'er dwalt in ae place.

Pride and laziness tak muckle uphauding.

Pride but profit soon gangs barefoot.

[*But,* without.]

Pride gaes afore a fa'

Pride never leaves its master till he gets a fa'.

Pride that dines wi' vanity sups wi' contempt.

PROPERTY.

A bird in the hand's worth twa in a bush.
Possession is eleven points o' the law.
The ill use we mak o' our prosperity is often the cause o' our
    misfortunes.

PRUDENCE IN ACTION.

A bite is aften better gien than eaten.
A penny saved is twice earned.
A sma' leak will sink a great ship.
Ane may like the kirk weel enough, and no ride on the rigging o't.
    ["A man may love a thing or person very well, and yet not show too much
    fondness." —*Kelly.*]
Be ready with your hat, but slow with your purse.
Be the thing ye wad be ca'd.
Be what you seem, and seem what you are.
Before you choose a friend eat a peck o' saut wi' him.
    [That you may be the better acquainted with his humours.]
Better at a time to gie than tak.
Better master ane than fight wi' ten.
Cast not out the auld water till the new come in.
Combat vice in the first attack, and ye'll come aff conqueror.
Count like Jews and gree like brithers.
Count siller after a' your kin.
Cut your coat according to your claith.
Deal sma' and sair a'.
Dinna cast awa the cog when the cow flings.
    [Leave other people's business alone.]
Get what you can, and keep what you hae, is the way to get rich.
Lay a thing by, and it will come o' use.
Let sleeping dogs lie.
Let weel alane.
Let your horse drink what he will, but not when he will.
Little meddling maks fair parting.
Lock your door that you may keep your neighbour honest.
Mak the best o' a bad bargain.
Mak your hay when the sun shines.
Never find fault wi' my shoon, unless you pay my souter.
Though auld and wise, yet still advise.
    [*Advise,* take advice.]
Wink at sma faults, ye hae great anes yoursel.
You'll ne'er harry yoursel wi' your ain hands.

PRUDENCE IN CONVERSATION.

A close mouth catches nae flies.

A gude tongue is a safe weapon.

A gude word is as easy said as an ill ane.

A man may haud his tongue in an ill time.

Ale-sellers should not be tale-tellers.

A' that's said in the kitchen, shouldna be tauld in the ha'.

A' the truth shouldna be tauld.

Believe not a' you hear, and tell not a' you believe.

He kens muckle wha kens when to speak, but far mair wha kens when to haud his tongue.

He that speaks the thing he shouldna, will hear the thing he wouldna.

It's a gude tongue that says nae ill, but a better heart that thinks nane.

Little said is soonest mended.

Seek muckle, get something; seek little, and get naething.

REPUTATION.

A gude name is sooner tint than won.

Better a gude name than a fou house.

Reputation is aften got without merit and tint without crime.

Reputation is to virtue what light is to a picture.

The first step to a gude name is a gude life, and the next step is gude behaviour.

They that get the name o' early rising, may lie in bed a' day.

RICHES.

A fou hand may count wi' the deil.

A fou purse maks a man speak.

A fou purse maks a tattling merchant.

A fou purse never lacks friends.

A gowd key will open ony lock.

A heavy purse maks a light heart.

A penny in my purse will gar me drink when my friends winna.

A penny in the purse is a merry companion.

A penny in the purse is better than a crown spent.

A rich man has mair cousins than his father had kin.

A rich man's wooing need seldom be a lang ane.

As wealth wanders, wit weakens.

A penny in the purse is a merry companion.

Be it better, be it worse, be ruled by him that has the purse.

Bear wealth, poverty will bear itself.

Gear is easier gotten than guided.

Gowd gets in at ilka yett except heaven.

Gowd is gude only in the hand o' virtue.

Leal folk ne'er wanted gear.

Little wealth, little sorrow.

Live within your income and live lang, is the sure way to get rich.

Money is aye welcome, were it in a dirty clout.

Money is better than my lord's letter.

Money is like the muck midden, it does nae gude till it be spread.

Money is the root o' a' ill.

Money maks the mare to go.

Money would beget, if there was money to get it.

Mony ane's gear is mony ane's death.

Money purses haud friends lang thegether.

Moyen does muckle, but money does mair.

Riches are got wi' pain, kept wi' care, and tint wi' grief.

Riches have made mair men covetous, than covetousness has made men rich.

Wealth as it is bestowed, and knowledge as it is communicated, properly constitute their value.

Wealth, like want, ruins mony.

When honour grew mercenary, riches grew honourable.

SELFISHNESS.

Every miller would weise the water to his ain mill.

Farmers' faugh gars lairds laugh.

> The meal cheap, and the shoon dear,
> The souter's wife likes weel to hear.

SELF-WILL.

A wilfu man maun hae his way.

A wilfu man should be unco wise.

He that winna be counselled canna be helped.

He wouldna gie an inch o' his ain will for a span o' his thrift.

Tak your ain will o't, and you'll no die o' the pet.

Tak your ain will o't, as the cat did o' the haggis—first at the haggis and then creepit into the bag.

You're as wilfu as a sow—you'll neither lead nor drive.

SLANDER.

A tale-bearer is waur than a thief.
A tale ne'er tines in the telling.
Our *bosom* friends are sometimes our backbiters.
Slander leaves a sair behind.

SORROW.

A sorrowfu' heart's aye dry.
　　[Applied to widows or widowers who drink freely to quench their grief.]
All earthly pleasures perish in sorrow.
Dool and an ill life soon mak an auld wife.
He's weel worth sorrow that buys't wi' his ain siller.
　　[*Worth,* deserving of.]
O' a' sorrows a fou sorrow is the best.
　　["Spoken when friends die and leave good legacies."—*Kelly.*]
Sorrow and ill weather come unsent for.
Time and thinking tame the strongest grief.
When sorrow comes, it runs.
When sorrow sleeps, wake it not.

STEALING.

A careless watch invites the thief.
Begin wi' needle and preen, and end wi' cow and ewe.
Begin wi' needle and preen, and end wi' horned nowte.
He that steals a preen, will steal a better thing.

TASTE.

Ae man's breath is anither man's death.
Ae man's meat is anither man's poison.
Fancy surpasseth beauty.
"Ilka ane to their taste," quo' the man, when he kissed his cow.
Ilka man as he likes, let him send to the cook.
　　[Let him choose as he pleases.]
It's no aye gude in the maw that's sweet in the mouth.
The proof o' the puddin's the preeing o't.
They that like the middin see nae motes in't.

THRIFTLESSNESS.

A fat kitchen is near to poverty.
Buy what you dinna want, and ye'll sell what you canna spare.
He eats the calf in the cow's wame.
[He spends his rent before it is due.]
He that borrows and biggs—maks feasts and thiggs—
—Drinks and is not dry,—these three are not thrifty.
He that spends his gear before he gets't, will hae little gude o't.
He that winna lout and lift a preen will ne'er be worth a groat.
He that winna save a penny will ne'er hae ony.
He wha spends before he thrives will beg before he thinks.
Spare at the spiggot, and let out at the bung hole.
[Penny wise and pound foolish.]

TRUTH

In our muckle clavering truth is tint.
There's mony a sooth word spoken in bourding.
Truth and oil are aye uppermost.
Truth has a gude face but raggit claes.
Truth is the dochter o' time.
Truth will aye stand without a prop.

VIRTUE.

Gold is beneficial only in the hands of virtue.
Search others for their virtues and yourself for your vices.
Virtue is above value.
Virtue is its ain reward.
Virtue that requires a guard is no worth a sentinel.

VISITORS, WELCOME AND UNWELCOME.

A constant guest is ne'er welcome.
Fresh fish, and unwelcome visitors, stink before they are three
    days auld.
He's as welcome as snaw in hairst.
He's as welcome as water in a riven ship.
He that comes unca'd sits unsair'd.
He that's welcome fares well.
His absence is gude company.
His room is better than his company.
Stay nae langer in a friend's house than you're welcome.

Fresh fish, and unwelcome visitors, stink before they are three days auld.

WAR.

War maks thieves, and peace hangs them.
When drums beat law is silent.

WASTE.

Biggin and bairns marrying are arrant wasters.
Haste maks waste, and waste maks want.
It's nae wonder wasters want and laithrons lag behind.
It's weel war'd that wasters want.
Kindle a candle at baith ends and it will soon burn out.

WISDOM.

A little wit sairs a lucky man.
A wife is wise aneugh wha kens her ain gudeman's breeks frae
    her ain kirtle.
    ["She is a good wife who knows the true measure of the husband's
    authority and her obedience."—*Kelly*.1]
A wise head maks a close mouth.
A wise man gets learning frae them that hae nane to themselves.
A wise man wavers, a fool is fixed.
An ounce o' a man's ain wit is worth ten o' ither folk's.
Better ae wit bought than twa for nought.
He has mair wit in his wee finger than ye hae in your hail
    bouk (body).
He's a wise bairn that kens his ain father.
He's a wise man wha can tak care o' himsel.
He's wise that can mak a friend o' a fae.
He who ne'er thinks will ne'er be wise.
He who serves God is the truly wise man.
Honest men marry soon, wise men never.
If misfortune maks us wise, it pays for our losses.
The greatest clerks are no the wisest men.
The less wit a man has, the less he kens the want o't.
Want o' wit is waur than want o' gear.
Wisdom is best taught by distress.
Wit ance bought is worth it twice taught.
Young men are made wise, auld men become so.

WOMAN.

A woman is at the best when she's openly bad.
A woman's gude either for something or naething.
A woman's mind is like the wind in a winter's night.
A woman's wark is ne'er done.
Frailty, thy name is Woman.
It's no 'What is she?' but 'What has she?'
Women and wine, dice and deceit, mak wealth sma and want
    great.
Women laugh when they can, and greet when they will.

WIVES.

A bonnie wife and a back door aften mak a man poor.
A fair wife without a tocher is like a fine house without furniture.
A grunting horse and a graining wife seldom fail their master.
> ["It is observed that tender and sickly wives commonly live long, and a
> horse that grunts under a man proves often very durable."—*Kelly.*]

    A horse broken and a wife to break,
    A horse made and a wife to make.
A house wi' a reek and a wife wi' a reard will mak a man rin to the
    door.
A toom pantry maks a thriftless gudewife.
An ill wife and a new lighted candle should hae their heads
    hauden down.
Auld wives and bairns mak fools o' physicians.
Auld wives were aye gude maidens.
Bad legs and ill wives ought to stay at home.
Breeding wives are aye greening.
Choose thy wife amang the virtuous, and thy friend among the
    wise.
Choose your wife on Saturday, and not on Sunday.
> [Choose her for her everyday usefulness rather than for her appearance
> on Sunday.]

Every man can guide an ill wife, but him that has her.
Fleas and a girning wife are wakerife bedfellows.
Greening wives are aye greedy.
The death o' your first wife made sic a hole in your heart that a'
    the rest slipped through.
    The gude or ill hap o' a gude or ill life,
    Is the gude or ill choice o' a gude or ill wife.
There's ae gude wife in the warld, and ilka ane thinks he has her.

Waes the wife that wants the tongue, but weels the man that gets her.

Wives and water-mills are aye wanting.

Wives and wind are necessary evils.

Wives maun be had, whether gude or bad.

 Wives maun hae their wills while they live,
 For they mak nane when they die.

You may drive the deil into a wife, but you'll ne'er ding him out o' her.

You would mak a gude wife—you haud the grip you get.

MAIDENS.

A dink maiden aft maks a dirty wife.

A fair maiden tocherless will get mae wooers than husbands.

A maid aft seen and a gown aft worn are disesteemed and held in . scorn.

A seven years' maiden is aye at the slight.

A tocherless dame stays lang at hame.

Ladies and turkeys need delicate upbringing.

Lasses and glasses are bruckle wares.

Like the lassies o' Bayordie, ye learn by the lug.

 Maidens should be mild and meek—
 Quick to hear, and slow to speak.

Maidens should be mim till they're married, and then they may burn kirks.

Maidens want naething but a husband, and then they want everything.

Maidens' bairns and bachelors' wives are aye weel bred.

Maidens' tochers, and ministers' stipends, are aye less than they're ca'd.

Mealy mou'd maidens stand lang at the mill.

WORTH.

If a gude man thrive, a' thrives wi' him.

The first step to virtue is to love it in anither.

The worth o' a thing is best kent by the want o't.

The worth o' a thing is what it will bring.

Virtue ne'er grows auld.

We ne'er ken the worth o' water till the well be dry.

Worth has been under-rated ever since wealth has been over-rated.

Worth may be blamed, but never shamed.

YOUTH.

A raggit cowte aft maks a noble aiver.
Raw dauds mak fat lads.
Reckless youth maks ruefu' age.
Royet lads mak sober men.
Rule youth weel, and age will rule itsel.
The laxy lad maks a stark auld man.

TRUISMS.

A bad wound may heal, but a bad name will kill.
A bald head is soon shaven.
A club foot winna mak a gude shinty.
A common blot is nae stain.
A constant guest is never welcome.
A cracket bell will never mend.
A craw is nae whiter for being washed.
A fou heart is aye kind.
A gien horse shouldna be looked in the mouth.
A groat is ill saved that shames its master.
A gude calf is better than a calf o' a gude kind.
A gude cow may hae an ill calf.
A gude word before is worth twa behind.
A gude word finds a gude place.
A gude year winna mak him, or an ill year break him.
   |A beggar will never be bankrupt.|
A guilty conscience needs nae accuser, a clear conscience fears
   nane.
A hen that lays thereout should hae a white nest-egg.
   |" A man given to extravagant amours in his single life has need to marry a
   handsome wife to keep him at home " Kelly|
A lang tongue has a short hand.
   |Those who promise most often do least.|
A man canna bear a' his ain kin about on his ain back.
A man has nae mair gudes than he gets gude o'.
A man may woo whare he will, but maun wed whare his weird is.
A man's hat in his hand ne'er did him harm.
A moudiewort needs nae lantern.
A muffled cat was ne'er a gude mouser.
A new pair o' breeks will cast down an auld doublet.
   |" Spoken when an old man marries a young woman." — Kelly|
A raggit coat is armour against the robber.
A scalded cat dreads cauld water.

A short grace is gude for hungry folk.

A taking hand will ne'er want, let the world be e'er sae scant.

A wild goose ne'er laid tame eggs.

A winter night, a woman's mind, and a laird's purpose aften change.

A wonder lasts but nine days, and then the puppy's een are open.

A word is enough to the wise.

Ae man may tak a horse to the water, but twenty winna gar him drink.

Ae rotten apple spoils its neighbour.

Ae scabbit sheep will smit a hail hirsell.

[Will infect a whole flock.]

Ae swallow doesna mak a simmer.

Ae turn weel done is twice done.

Ae vice is more expensive than mony virtues.

After a storm comes a calm

After clouds comes fair weather.

An auld horse may die waiting for the grass.

An auld pock is aye skailing.

An auld sack needs muckle clouting.

An eating horse ne'er foundered.

An honest occupation is the best patrimony.

An ill turn is soon done.

Ane may like a haggis weel enough that would not like the bag bladded on his chafts.

As ane flits anither sits, and that maks mailings dear.

As gude eat the deil as sup the kail he's boiled in.

As gude merchants tine as win.

As lang lasts the hole as the heal-leather.

[A reply to those who direct attention to a hole in your shoe.]

As many castles hae been ta'en by clemency as cruelty.

As the market gaes, the wares maun sell.

As ye brew sae maun you drink.

Auld tods need nae tutors.

Avoid in yoursel what you blame in ithers.

Bannocks are better than nae bread.
'Because' is a woman's reason.
Bees that hae honey in their mouths hae stings in their tails.
Beef-steaks and porter is gude belly mortar.
Better a bite in the morning than fast a' day.
Better a finger aff than aye wagging.
Better a gude fame than a fair face.
Better a sair tae than a fause friend.
Better a sma fish than a empty dish.
Better be alane than in ill company.
Better be at the end o' a feast than at the beginning o' a fray.
Better be envied than pitied.
Better be friends at a distance than enemies at hame.
Better be kind than cumbersome.
Better be merry and spend a' than sad and hain naething.
Better be merry wi' something than sad wi' naething.
Better be the head o' the commons than the tail o' the gentry.
Better do it than wish it done.
Better eat grey bread in youth than in eild.
Better be fed than bred.
Better flatter a fool than fight him.
Better gang to bed supperless than rise in debt.
Better gie the slight than tak it.
Better gude sale than gude ale.
Better hae than want.
Better half egg than toom doup.
> [Than an empty shell.]

Better hands loose than in ill tethering.
Better happy at court than in good service.
Better haud wi' the hound than rin wi' the hare.
> ["Better be able to grapple with a difficulty than to have a probability to escape it."—*Kelly*.]

Better idle than ill employed.
Better keep weel than mak weel.
Better late thrive than ne'er do weel.
Better my bairns seek frae me, than I frae my bairns.
Better play for nought than work for nought.
Better plays the fou wame than the new coat.
> ["A child will be more cheerful upon being well-fed than new clothed."—*Kelly*.]

Better ride on an ass that carries you, than a horse that throws you.
Better rue sit than rue flit.
> [Better to remain where we are than to repent of removing.]

Better saucht wi' little aught than care wi' mony cows.

[Better peace and comfort with little belonging to us than care with much wealth.]

Better say 'Here it is' than 'Here it was.'

Better skaiths saved than mends made.

[Better damage not done than reparation made for damage inflicted.]

Better sma fish than nae fish.

Better spared than ill spent.

Better the barn filled than the bed.

Better to leave than want.

Better to sit still than rise and get a fa'.

Better twa skaiths than ae sorrow.

[Losses may be repaired, but sorrow may break the heart.]

Better unborn than untaught.

Better wade back mid water than gang forward and be drowned.

Bitter your foot slip than your tongue.

Better pills may hae blessed effects.

Bluid's thicker than water.

Busy folk are aye meddling.

Buy what ye dinna want, and ye'll sell what ye canna spare.

Censure is the tax a man pays to the public for being eminent.

Changes o' wark is a lightening o' hearts.

Charity begins at hame.

Clawing is bad: it begins wi' pleasure and ends wi' pain.

Clippet sheep will grow again.

Come when ye're ca'd, and ye'll no be chidden.

Command your passions, or they will command you.

Daub yoursel wi' honey and ye'll ne'er want flies.

Daylight will keek through a sma hole.

Dead men are freed men.

Eagles flee alane, but sheep herd thegither.

Equity judgeth with lenity, law with severity.

Every bird thinks its ain nest best.

Every man has his weak side.

Every man kens best whare his ain sair lies.

Every thing is the waur o' the wear.

Evil words cut mair than swords.

Evil words scald not the tongue.

Fair hair may hae foul roots.

Fairly and saftly gaes far journeys.

Four-and-twenty tailors canna mak a man.

Great bodies move slowly.

Greatness may big the monument, but goodness maun gie the epitaph.

Great pains and little gains soon mak a man weary.

Great tochers makna aye the greatest testaments.

Gude men are the masters o' their pleasures, bad men are the slaves o' theirs.

Hame is a hamely name.

Hankering and hanging on is but a poor trade.

He can ill rin that canna gang.

He is the slave o' a' slaves wha serves nane but himsel.

He's a fool that forgets himsel.

He's a gentle horse that ne'er threw his rider.

He's a gude gunner that aye hits the mark.

He's a silly body that's never missed.

He's a silly chield that can neither do nor say.

He that avoids temptation avoids the sin.

He that blaws in the stour fills his ain een.

> He that buys land buys stanes;
> He that buys beef buys banes;
> He that buys nuts buys shells;
> He that buys good ale buys naething else.

He that deceives me ance, shame fa' him; he that deceives me twice, shame fa' me.

He that does bidden deserve nae dinging.

He that draw his sword agains his prince may throw awa the scabbard.

He that grapes in the dark may fyle his fingers.

He that has a gude crap may bear wi' some thistles.

He that has but ae ee maun tent it weel.

He that has gowd may buy land.

He that has the langest sword is aye thought in the right.

He that has twa hoards is able to get a third.

He that hews aboon his head may get a spale in his ee.

[He that aims at things beyond his power may be ruined by his project.]

He that's far frae his gear is near to his skaith.

He that lends money to a friend has a double loss.

[Because he loses both his money and his friend.]

He that lippens to chance lippens his back to a slap.

He that lippens to lent ploughs, his land will lie lea.

He that lives in a glass house shouldna cast stones at his neighbour.

He that oppresses honesty ne'er had any.
He that pays last ne'er pays twice.
He that pities another minds himsel.
He that says what he likes will hear what he doesna like.
He that sells his wares for words maun live on wind.
He that shows his purse bribes the thief.
He that sleeps wi' dogs maun rise wi' flaes.
[He that keeps bad company will be the worse for it.]
He that speaks to himsel speaks to a fool.
He that spits against the wind spits in his ain face.
He that swims in sin will sink in sorrow.
He that tholes overcomes.
He that waits for a dead man's shoon gaes lang barefit.
He that wants content canna sit easy in his chair.
He that wears black maun wear a brush on his back.
He that would pu' the sweet rose maun sometimes be scarted wi'
    the thorns.
Hope is the dream o' a waking man.

I can see as far into a millstane as he that picked it.
I could hae done that mysel, but no sae weel.
I'll no tell a lie for scant o' news.
I'll pay you and put naething in your pouch.
[I'll give you a thrashing.]
'I winna mak a toil o' a pleasure,' quo' the man when he buried
    his wife.
If youth knew what age would crave, it would baith get and save.
Ifs and Ands spoil mony a gude charter.
It's a sair time when the mouse looks out o' the meal barrel wi'
    the tear in its ee.
It's a sooth dream that's seen waking.
It's a sort of favour to be denied at first.
It's a sour reek when the gudewife dings the gudeman.
It's gude to begin weel, but better to end weel.
It's gude to hae your cog out when it rains kail.
[Make hay while the sun shines.]
It's ill 'praising green barley.
['praising, valuing, setting a price upon.]
It's ill kitchen that keep the bread awa.
It's nae play when ane laughs and anither greets.
It's needless to bed a wren rin.
It's needless to mak twa bites o' a cherry.
It's needless to pour water on a drowned mouse.
It's ne'er ower late for repentance.

Its a sair time when the mouse looks oot a' the meal barrell wi' a tear in its e'e.

Its weel your thoughts are no written on your forehead.

It's no a' gowd that glitters.

It's no the rumbling cart that fa's first ower the brae.

[It's not the likeliest person that dies first.]

It's no tint that comes at last.

It's ower late to cast the anchor when the ship's on the rock.

It's ower late to jouk when the head's aff.

It's ower late to lout when the head's got a clout.

It's weel your faults are no written on your forehead.

It may be true what some men say, but it maun be true what a'
men say.

It was ne'er a gude aiver that flung at the broose.

It would be a hard task to follow a black dockit sow through a
burnt moor this night.

It would do a blind man gude to see't.

Keep your tongue a prisoner, and your body will gang free.

Lacking breeds laziness, but praise breeds pith.

Laith to bed, laith to rise.

Lang fasting gathers wind.

Lang lean maks hamald cattle.

Lang or you cut Falkland Wood wi' a penknife.

[Said when people begin a work without proper tools, or enter upon a large
undertaking without sufficient means.]

Langest at the fire soonest finds cauld.

Lean liberty is better than fat slavery.

Listen at a hole, and ye'll hear news o' yoursel.

Little and often fills the purse.

Little gear is soon spent.

Little meddling maks fair parting.

Little wit in the head maks muckle travel to the heel.

[Unskilful persons put themselves to more trouble than is necessary.]

May he that turns the clod ne'er want a bannock.

Meddle wi' your match.

Meat and measure mak a' men wise.

Men speak o' the fair as things went there.

Mocking is catching.

Mony ane blames their wife for their ain unthrift.

Listen at a hole, and ye'll hear news o' yoursel.

Mony ane would blush to hear what they are no ashamed to do.
Mony ane wytes their wife for their ain thoughtless life.
Mony fair promises at the marriage-making, but few at the
    tocher paying.
Mony gude nights laith awa.
Mony hands mak light wark.
Mony irons in the fire, some maun cool.
Mony says 'weel' when it ne'er was waur.
Mony ways o' killing a dog without hanging him.
Mony words would hae muckle drink.
Muckle gude may it do you and merry go down, with every lump
    as big as my thumb.
Muckle maun a gude heart thole.

Nae fleeing without wings.
Nae force against the flail.
Nae man is wise at a' times, nor wise on a' things.
Nae man likes fetters, though they be forged in gowd.
Nae mills, nae meal.
Nae siller, nae service.
Naething dries sae fast as a woman's tears.
Naething enters into a close neive.
Naething is ill said, if it's no ill taen.
Naething sooner maks a man look auld, than sitting ill to his
    meat.
    [*To sit ill to one's meat,* to be ill fed.]
Nane can play the fool sae weel as a wise man.
Nature passeth nurture.
Need maks virtue.
Never venture, never win.
New lairds hae new laws.
Night is the mither o' thoughts.

O' a' trades, the poet is fondest o' his wark.
O' little meddling comes muckle care.
Opportunities mak a thief.
Our first breath is the beginning o' death.

Practice maks perfectness.
Put the poor man's penny and the rich man's penny in ae purse,
    and they'll draw thegither.
Put the poor man's penny and the rich man's penny in ae purse,
    and they'll come out alike.

Reek follows the fairest, bear witness to the crook.
> [Excellence is accompanied by envy.]

Right mixture maks gude mortar.

Right, Rab: swine are gude mutton.

Right wrangs nae man.

Rome wasna built in ae day.

Say aye 'No,' and ye'll ne'er be married.

Saying gangs cheap.

> Say weel and do weel, end wi' ae letter:
> Say weel is gude, but do weel is better.

Scarting and nipping is Scotch folks' wooing.

Scotchmen are aye wise ahint the hand.

Scotchmen aye reckon frae an ill hour.

Scotchmen aye tak their mark frae mischief.
> [Reckon from the occurrence of an accident or other misfortune.]

Second thoughts are best.

> Seek muckle and get something.
> Seek little and get naething.

Seek till you find, and ye'll no lose your labour.

Show me the guest that the house is the war o'.

Show me the man, and I'll show you the law.

Shod in the cradle and barefit in the stable.

Slow fires mak sweet meat.

Smooth waters runs deepest.

Sodgers, fire, and water soon mak room for themsels.

Speech is the midwife o' the mind.

Spit in your loof, and haud fast.

Spit on a stane and it will weet at last.

Spit on 't, and ca 't thegither wi' a stane.

Stown dunts are sweetest.

Strike as you feed, and that's but soberly.

Stuffing haud out the storm.
> ["Advising men to take some good thing before they travel in a bad day."—*Kelly.*]

Stay and drink you browst.
> ["Take a share of the mischief that you have occasioned."—*Kelly.*]

Sticking gangs not by strength, but by the right use o' the gully.

Tak part o' the pelf when the pack is a-dealing.

Tak your will o't, as the cat did o' the haggis.

Take your will, you're wise enough.

Tear ready, tail ready.

That's the best gown that gaes up and down the house.
The banes bear the beef hame.
The best is aye the cheapest.
The cow may die ere the grass grow.
The cow may want her tail yet.
  ["You may want my kindness hereafter though you deny me yours
  now."—*Kelly.*]
The cure may be waur than the disease.
The day has een, the night has lugs.
The deil's journeyman ne'er want wark.
The dorty dame may fa' in the dirt.
The farer ben the welcomer—(Highland hospitality.)
The higher you climb, the greater the fa'.
The horse shoe that clatters wants a nail.
The langest day will hae an end.
The man may eithly tine a stot that canna count his kine.
The mither's breath is aye sweet.
The moudiewort feedsna on midges.
The muck midden is the mither o' the meal kist.
The shortest road is whare the company is gude.
The simple man's the beggar's brither.
The smith's mare, and the souter's wife, are aye warst shod.
The snail is as soon at its rest as the swallow.
The still sow eats up the draff.
The stout horse gets aye the hard wark.
The sun is nae waur for shining on the midden.
The wolf may lose his teeth, but never his nature.
There are mair knavery by sea and land than a' the earth besides.
There are mair knaves in my kin than honest men in yours.
There are mair married than gude house hauders.
There are mair wark days than life days.
There are mair ways than ane o' keeping the craws frae the
  stack.
There are nane sae weel shod but may slip.
There are three things in a' things.
There belangs mair to a bed than four bare legs.
There belangs mair to a ploughman than whistling.
There grows nae grass at the market-cross.
There's a gude and a bad side in every thing: a' the art is to find it
  out.
There's a time to gley, and a time to look even.
There's an end o' a lang story.
There's as gude fish in the sea as ever cam out o't.

There's little for the rake after the shool.

There's nae iron sae hard but rust will fret it.

There's nae claith sae fine but moths will eat it.

There's nae sport whare there's neither auld folk nor bairns.

There's nae sun sae bright but clouds will owercast it.

There's nae woo sae course but it will tak some colour.

There's ower mony nicks in your horn.

[You're far too cunning.]

There's naething comes out o' an oulie pig but an ill smell.

[*Oulie pig*, an oil vessel.]

There's naething sae like an honest man as an arrant knave.

There's nane deceived but them wha trust.

There's nane sae blind as them that winna see.

They're no a' saints that get the name o't.

They're scarce o' horse-flesh that ride on the dog.

They hae nae need o' a turnspit that hae only an egg to their dinner.

They hae need o' a canny cook that hae but ae egg to their dinner.

They need muckle that naething will content.

They ne'er saw a haggis wha think a puddin a feast.

They that drink langest live langest.

They that live langest fetch wood farest.

They that see you in daylight winna rin awa wi' you in the dark.

They that see you in daylight winna break the house for you at night.

[The two preceding spoken to ugly women.]

Tramp on a worm and it will turn.

[The meanest when injured will shew resentment.]

Twa blacks winna mak a white.

'Twa heads are better than ane,' as the wife said, when she and her dog gaed to the market.

Twa heads are better than ane, though they were only sheep heads.

Whare the deer's slain the bluid will lie.

Whare there's muckle courtesy there's little kindness.

What is gotten ower the deil's back is spent below his belly.

What we love heartily, we love smartly.

What winna mak a pat may mak a pat lid.

When the barn's fou, you may thrash at the door.

When the burn does not babble, it's either ower toom or ower fu'.

When the craw flies, her tail follows.

When the dike's laighest, it's easiest loupit.

When the heart's past hope, the face is past shame.

When the horse is at the gallop the bridle's ower late.

When the tod gets to the wood, he caresna wha keeks at his tail.

Wide lugs and a short tongue are best.

Wise men are caught wi' wiles.

Wishers and woulders are poor householders.

Woo sellers ken aye woo buyers.

Work for naething maks folk dead-swear.

Work legs and win legs, hain legs and tine legs.

Ye're as white as a loan soup.

[*Loan soup*, milk fresh from the cow. Said to flatterers, who are called *White folks*.]

Ye're black about the mou for want o' kissing.

Ye're buttoned up the back like achmahoy's dog.

[Said to lean people whose back bones stand out.]

Ye're like me, and I'm like sma drink.

[That is, little worth.]

Ye're like the smith's dog, ye sleep at the sound o' the hammer, and waken at the crunching o' teeth.

Ye're mista'en o' the stuff—it's half silk.

Ye're ower bird-mou'd (mealy-mouthed).

Ye canna sell the cow and sup the milk too.

Ye canna wash a black man white.

Ye gie gude counsel, but he's a fool that taks it.

Ye had aye gude whittle at your belt.

[Said to them that have a ready answer.]

Ye hae a sa' for a' sairs.

Ye hae come in time for tineing a darg.

[For losing a day's work, that is, too late.]

Ye hae got baith the skaith and the scorn.

Ye hae missed that, as you did your mither's blessing.

Ye may gape lang ere a bird flee in your mouth.

Ye may tine the father seeking the son.

Ye may wash aff dirt but no dun hide.

Ye needna blame God if the deil ding you ower.

Ye needna lay thereout for want o' a nest egg.

[Spoken to him that has a handsome young wife.]

Ye strive about uncoft gaits (unbought goats).

Ye tak mair in your mouth than your cheeks will haud.

Ye wad gar me trew my head was cow'd, and I find the hair on't.

Ye'll do little for God, if the deil was dead.

Ye'll gang a grey gate.

[You will take a wicked course.]

Ye'll gather nae gowd aff windlestraes.

Ye'll get as muckle for ae wish this year, as for twa fernyear (last year.)

[That is, nothing.]

Ye'll get nae mair o' a cat but the skin.

Ye'll get waur bodes ere Beltane.

[Ye'll get worse offers before the 1st of May.]

Ye'll kythe in your ain colours yet.

MISCELLANEOUS.

A daft nurse maks a wise wean.

A day to come seems langer than a year that's gane.

A dear ship lies lang in the harbour.

[Applied often to maids that are fastidious.]

A dog's life—hunger and ease.

A hairy man's a geary man, but a hairy wife's a witch.

A laughing faced lad maks a lither servant.

[Because he is too full of roguery to be diligent.]

A man o' mony trades begs his bread on Sunday.

A man's mind is a mirk mirror.

A man, like a watch, is valued for his time.

A pair o' heels is worth twa pair o' hanns.

As lang as a dog would be bound wi' a bluid puddin.

As lang runs the fox as he has feet.

As plain as the nose on your face.

As sair fights the wren as the crane.

As soon comes the lamb's skin to the market as the auld sheep's.

As tired as a tyke is o' langkail.

Bachelor's wives and maidens bairns are aye weel bred.

Be either a man or a mouse.

Be gaun, the gate's before you.

[A cool farewell.]

Be not a baker if your head be o' butter.

Bread and cheese is gude to eat,
When folk can get nae ither meat.

Break my head and then draw on my how.

Bridal feasts are soon forgotten.

Bridal feuds are soon forgotten.

By chance a cripple may catch a hare.

Ca' again, you're no a ghaist.
[Your visits are welcome.]
Ca' canny and flee laigh.
Ca' canny, and ye'll break nae graith.
Ca' me and I'll ca' thee.
[Speak well of me, and I'll speak well of you.]
Claw me and I'll claw thee.
[Promote my interests, and I'll promote yours.]
Clawing and eating needs but a beginning.
Clean pith and fair play.
Cocks are aye gude will'd o horses' corn.
Come a' to Jock Fool's house, and ye'll get bread and cheese.
Come back the morn and ye'll get pies for naething.

Daffin and want o' wit, maks auld wives donnart.
Dame, deem warily, ye watna wha wytes yoursel.
[*Deem,* judge.]
Dawted dochters mak dawly wives.
Death at the ae door, and herschip at the tither.
Dear bought and far sought, is meat for ladies.
Deil be in the house that ye're beguiled in.
[It would take the deil to cheat you.]
Deil be in the pock that ye cam in.
Double charges rive cannons.
[Said when more is pressed upon one than he can bear.]
Dows and dominies aye leave a foul house.
[*Dows,* pigeons, which dirty everything where they are.]

Eagles catch nae flies.
Early pricks will be thorns.
Ease and honour are seldom bedfellows.
Either live or die wi' honour.
Enough is as gude as a feast.
Even as you win 't, sae may you wear 't.
Ever spare, ever bare.
Every ane bows to the bush that beilds him.
[Every man pays court to him who gives him protection.]
Every ane for himsel, and God for us a'.
Every ane has his ain draff pock, though some hang sider than
    ithers.
[Every man has his faults, though some have more than others.]
Every ane loups the dike at the laighest.
'Every ane to his ain trade,' quo' the brewster to the bishop.

Every day is no Yule day: cast the cat a castock.

[Every day is not Christmas day, therefore be more liberal than usual.]

Every dream o' delight has a pound o' spite.

Every dud bids anither gude day.

[Said of people in rags and tatters.]

Every inch o' joy has an ell o' annoy added to it.

Every man's blind in his ain case.

For fashion's sake, as the dogs gang to the market.

For gude cheese and gude cheer mony haunt the house.

Force without foresight is little worth.

Forced prayers are no gude for the soul.

Forewarned, half armed.

Fou o' courtesy, fou o' craft.

Foul fa' nought, and then he'll get naething.

[Said contemptuously of those who are presumptuous in their expectations.]

Foul water will slocken fire.

Frae the teeth forward.

[Not from the heart.]

Friday flit, short time sit.

[The day being considered unlucky.]

Gane is the goose that laid the muckle egg.

Gaunting bodes wanting ane o' things three—sleep, meat, or gude companie.

Gaunting bodes wanting ane o' things three—sleep, meat, or making o'.

Gaunting gaes frae man to man.

Gar wood is ill to grow, chuckie stanes are ill to chow.

Gaylie would be better.

Gentle servants are poor men's hardships.

Gentle servants are rich men's tinsel.

Gentlemen are unco scant, when a wabster gets a lady.

Gibbie's grace—deil claw the clungest.

Gie a carl your finger and he'll tak your hail hand.

Gie a dog an ill name and he'll soon be hanged.

Gie a gaun man a drink and a rising man a knock.

Gie a greedy dog a muckle bane.

Gie a strong thief a stark name.

Gie a thing, tak a thing, and that's the ill man's ring.

[*Ill man*, the devil.]

Hang a thief when he's young, and he'll no steal when he's auld.

Hang him that has nae shift, and hang him that has ower mony.

[The former is not worth hanging, the latter cannot be hanged too soon.]

Hang hunger, and drown drouth.

Hanging is nae better than it's ca'd.

Happy go lucky.

[At all hazards.]

Happy is the bride that the sun shines on;
Happy is the corpse that the rain rains on.

Happy man be his dool.

Happy man, happy kavel.

Hardships seldom come single.

Haud your hand, your father slew a whaup.

[In ridicule of those that threaten yet dare not execute.]

He begs frae them that borrowed frae him.

He blaws in her lug fu' brawly.

[*Blaw in one's lug,* to flatter one extravagantly.]

He brings a staff to break his ain head.

He can do ill, and he may do gude.

He caresna whase bairns greet, if his laugh.

I had but little butter, and I cast it on the coals.

[The little I had I mismanaged.]

I hae a gude sword, but it's in the castle.

I hae gotten an ill kame for my ain hair.

[I have entered upon a troublesome business.]

I hae ither fish to fry.

I hae ither tow on my roke.

I hae mair to do than a dish to wash.

I hae muckle to do, and few to do for me.

I hae seen as fou a haggis toom'd on the midden.

[I have seen people as rich brought to poverty. Another explanation is, I
have seen as good an article thrown away.]

If you dinna haud him, he'll do't a'.

[A taunt to a lazy fellow.]

If you dinna like what I gie you, tak what you brought wi' you.

If you dinna steal my kail, break not down my dike.

If you had stuck a knife in my heart, it wadna hae bled.

[I was so much surprised.]

If you laugh at your ain sport, the company will laugh at you.

If you like the nut, crack it.

Keek in the stoup was ne'er a gude fellow.

Keep the head and the feet warm, and the rest will tak nae harm.

Keep your ain crease for your ain cart-wheels.

Keep your breath to cool your crowdie.

[Said to them who talk a great deal to little purpose.]

Keep your mocks till you're married.

Keep your kiln-dried taunts for your mouldy haired maidens.

Keep your mouth shut and your een open.

Keep your tongue within your teeth.

Ken yoursel, and your neighbours winna mistak you.

Little Jock gets the little dish, and that keeps him lang little.

["Poor people are poorly served, which prolongs their poverty."—*Kelly.*]

Little ken'd and less cared for.

Little kens the auld wife, as she sits by the fire, what the wind is doing on Hurley-Burley-Swire.

["Hurle-burle-swyre is a passage through a ridge of mountains that separate Nithsdale from Twadale and Clydsdale: where the mountains are so indented; one with another, that there is a perpetual blowing. The meaning is, that they who are at ease know little of the trouble that others are exposed to."—*Kelly.*]

Little may an auld horse do, if he mayna neicher.

Little to fear when traitors are true.

Little troubles the ee, but less the soul.

Little winning maks a light purse.

Live upon love, as laverocks do on leeks.

Loud cheeps the mouse, when the cat's no rustling.

[When the cat's away the mice will play.]

Loud coos the dow, when the hawk's no whistling.

Mak a kiln o't, and creep in at the logie.

Mak a virtue o' necessity.

Mak not twa mows o' ae dochter.

Mak the best o' a bad bargain.

Malice is aye mindful.

Ne'er say Go, but gang.

Ne'er show your teeth unless you can bite.

Ne'er strive against the stream.

Ne'er take a forehammer to break an egg, when a nap wi' a knife will do.

Ne'er throw the bridle o' your horse ower a fool's arm.

Ne'er use the taws when the gloom will do.

Loud cheeps the Mouse when the cat's no rustling —
When the cat's away the mice will play.

Ne'er was a wife weel pleased coming frae the mill but ane, and
 she brak her neck bane.
Ne'er waur happen you than your ain prayer.
Nineteen naesays is half a grant.
Now is now, and Yule's in winter.

Of a' the meat i' the warld drink gaes best down.
On painting and fighting look adreich.
On the 25th October, there's ne'er a souter sober.
 [St. Crispin's day.]
'Onything becomes a gude face,' quo' the monkey, when he
 looked himsel i' the glass.
Our bosom friends are sometimes our backbiters.
Out o' sight out o' mind.
  Out o' the peat-pat into the mire:
  Out o' the frying pan into the fire.
Out on the highgate is aye fair play.
 [Honesty is the best policy.]
Ower fine a purse to put a plack in.
 [Said of a splendid house on a small estate.]
Ower holy was hanged, but rough and sonsy wan awa.
Ower muckle cookery spoils the brochan.
Ower strong meat for your weak stamach.
 [Said to old men when they marry young girls.]

Pay him hame in his ain coin.
Penny wise, and pound foolish.
Pigs may whistle, but they hae an ill mouth for't.
 [Such a thing is very unlikely.]
Pith is gude at a' plays but threading o' needles.
Poor folk seek meat for their stamachs, and rich folk stamachs
 for their meat.
Provision in season maks a rich house.
Puddins and paramours should be hetly handled.
Puddins and wort are hasty dirt.
Pu' the rose and leave the thorn.
Put on your spurs, and be at your speed.
Put the saddle on the right horse.
Put your shanks in your thanks, and mak gude gramashes o'
 them.
 [An answer to those that offer only thanks for payment.]

Quey calfs are dear veal.

[Because they should be kept for stock.]

Quietness is best.

Ripe fruit is soonest rotten.

Rob Peter to pay Paul.

Roose the fair day at e'en.

[Wait for the result of the project before you praise it.]

Roose the ford as ye find it.

Rue and thyme grow baith in ae garden.

'Saft beddin's gude for sair banes,' quo' Howie, when he streekit
    himsel on the midden head.

Sair yoursel, and your friends will think the mair o' you.

Sair yoursel till your bairns grow up.

'Saut,' quo' the souter, when he had eaten a' the cow but the tail.

["Spoken to them that flag, when they have almost finished a difficult
task."—*Kelly.*]

See for love and buy for siller.

Send you to the sea, and ye wouldna get saut water.

["Spoken when people foolishly come short of their errand."—*Kelly.*]

Set a thief to catch a thief.

Set your knee to't and right it.

Shame fa' the dog, that when he hunted you, didna gar you rin
    faster.

She brak her elbock on the kirk door.

[Said of an industrious maiden when she becomes a lazy wife.]

She frisks about like a cat's tail i' the sun.

She has an ill paut wi' her hind foot.

[She is stubborn.]

She hauds up her gab like an awmous dish.

She hauds up her head like a hen drinking water.

She's greeting at the thing that she laughed at fern-year.

[She is in labour.]

She's no to be made a sang about.

["An abatement to a woman's commendation for beauty."—*Kelly.*]

There was a wife wha kept her supper for her breakfast, and she
    died ere day.

'They're a bonny pair,' as the craw said o' his legs.

They're aye gude will'd o' their horse that hae nane.

They're far behind that may not follow.

They're keen o' company that taks the dog on their back.

They ne'er gae wi' the spit but they gat wi' the ladle.

> [They never gave anything without getting a return for it.]

They ne'er saw a haggis that think a puddin a feast.

They ne'er saw dainties that think a haggis a feast.

They that bourd wi' cats, maun count on scarts.

They that burn you for a witch will lose their coals.

They that finds keeps, they that losses seeks.

They were never fain that fidged, nor fou that licket dishes.

They were never first at the wark wha bade God speed the wark.

They wist as weel wha didna speir.

This and better may do, but this and waur will ne'er do.

Thoughts are free, and though I say little, I yerk at the thinking.

Thoughts beguile maidens, and sae fares wi' you that's nane.

Threatened folk live lang.

Three can keep a secret if twa be awa.

Whelps are aye blind that dogs get in haste.

Whiles you, and whiles me, sae gaes the baillierie.

> ["Spoken when persons or parties get authority by turns."—*Kelly.*]

Whitely things are aye tender.

Wonder at your auld shoon, when you hae gotten your new.

> ["An answer to them that say they wonder at you or what you do."—*Kelly.*]

Words are but wind, but dunts are the deil.

Work in God's name, and sae doesna the deil.

Ye're a corby messenger.

> [A messenger who returns not at all or too late, alluding to the raven in Noah's ark.]

Ye're a deil and nae cow like the man's bull.

Ye're a foot behind the foremost.

Ye're a gude seeker but an ill finder.

Ye're a maiden marrowless.

Ye're a man among geese when the gander's awa.

Ye're a rich rogue wi' twa sark and a rag.

Ye're a sweet nut for the deil to crack.

Ye're a' blawing like a bursten haggis.

Ye're a' out o't and into strae.

> [Quite mistaken.]

Ye're ane o' Cow-meek's breed, you'll stand without a bonoch.

Ye're an honest man and I'm your uncle, and that's twa great lies.

Ye're as daft as ye're days auld.

Ye're as lang tuning your pipes as anither would play a spring.
[You're as long in setting about a thing, as another would do it.]

Ye're a mim as a May puddock.

Ye're as muckle as half a witch.

Ye're at the lug o' the law.
[Ready to catch at what's going.]

WEATHER AND SEASONS.

CANDLEMAS-DAY.

If Candlemas day be fair and bright,
Winter will hae anither flight.
If Candlemas day hae showers and rain,
Winter is past, and will not come again.
When Candlemas day is come and gane,
The snaw lies on a het stane.
The shepherd would as lief see his wife on a bier,
As a Candlemas day to be pleasant and clear.
If Candlemas day be clear and fair,
The half o' winter's to come and mair:
If Candlemas day be dark and foul,
The half o' winter's past at Yule.
On Candlemas day you maun hae
Half your hay, and half your strae.
As lang as the bird sings before Candlemas, as lang it sings after Candlemas.

MARCH.

March winds and May sun
Mak claes white and lasses dun.
March comes in wi' an adder's head, and gangs out wi' a peacock's tail.
March comes like a lion, and gaes out like a lamb.
March grass never did gude.
March whisker ne'er was a gude fisher.
[A windy March is unfavourable to the angler.]

A windy March ne'er was a gude fish year.
A peck o' March dust is worth a king's ransom.
A peck o' March dust is worth a peck o' gowd.
 Sae mony mists in March ye see,
 Sae mony frosts in May will be.
On the 22nd o' March, the day and the night marches.

THE FURTUCH, OR BORROWING DAYS.

(The Last Three Days of March, Old Style.)

March borrows frae April three days, and they are ill;
April borrows frae March again, three days o' wind and rain.

 March said to April,
  Lend me days three;
 I see three hogs (sheep) upon yon hill,
  I'll try to gar them dee.
 The first day was wind and weet;
 The second day was snaw and sleet;
 The third day was sic a freeze,
 It froze the bird's nebs to the trees:—
But when the three days were come and gane,
The three little hoggies cam toddling hame.

APRIL.

The first day of April, send the gowk anither mile.
April showers bring milk and meal.
April showers bring summer flowers.
When April blaws his horn, it is gude for hay and corn.
The third day of April brings the gowk and nightingale.

MAY AND JUNE.

May showers bring milk and meal.
May floods ne'er did good.
 A peck o' March dust and a shower in May
 Maks the corn green and the fields look gay.
 A wet May and a windy
 Maks a fou barnyard and a findy.

Come it ear or come it late, in May will come the cow-quake.
　　Look at your corn in May,
　　And ye'll come weeping away:
　　Look at the same in June,
　　And ye'll be in anither tune.
　A leeking May and a warm June,
　Brings on the har'est very soon.
Cast ne'er a clout till May be out.
Barnaby bright, the langest day and the shortest night.
　　[St. Barnabas's Day, June 11th.]

JULY AND AUGUST.

　　If St. Swithin greets, the proverb says,
　　The weather will be foul for forty days.
As St. Swithin's day is fair or foul, sae is the weather for forty
　days.
　　[St. Swithin's day, July 15th.]
A shower of rain in July, when the corn begins to fill,
Is worth a plough of owsen, and a' belangs theretill.
　　If the first of July be rainy weather,
　　It will rain mair or less for four weeks together.
After Lammas corn ripens as much by night as by day.
　　If the twenty-fourth of August be fair and clear,
　　Then hope for a prosperous autumn that year.

DRY AND WET.

A dry simmer ne'er made a dry peck.
Drouth ne'er bred dearth.
Under water dearth; under snaw bread.
　　[Snow protects the seed or young grain, much rain spoils it.]
A Scotch mist will weet an Englishman to the skin.
He that wad hae a bad day may gang out in a fog after a frost.
　　When the mist is on the hill,
　　Then gude weather it doth spill:
　　When the mist taks to the sea,
　　Then gude weather it will be.
　An evening red and a morning grey
　Doth betoken a bonnie day:
　An evening grey and a morning red,
　Put on your hat or ye'll weet your head.

A rainbow in the morning is the sailor's warning.
A rainbow at noon will bring rain very soon.
A rainbow at night is the shepherd's delight.
If there be a rainbow in the eve, it will rain and leave.
If there be a rainbow in the morrow, it will neither lend nor
    borrow.
Clear in the south beguiled the cadger.
In the auld moon a cloudy morning bodes a fair afternoon.
A Saturday's moon, if it comes but ance in seven years, comes
    ower often.

SOWING AND HARVEST.

It's time to mak the bear-seed when the plane-tree covers the
    craw.
    When the slae-bush is as white as a sheet,
    Saw your bear, whether it be dry or weet.
Saw wheat in dirt, and rye in dust.
    The spring evenings are lang and teuch.
    The har'est evenings are soon ower the heugh.
In har'est the lairds are labourers.

WINTER.

As the day lengthens the cauld strengthens.
Winter's thunder bodes Simmer's hunger.
    Winter's thunder and Simmer's flood,
    Ne'er boded Scotland good.

WINDS.

When the wind's in the west, the weather's at the best.
When the wind's in the east, it's neither gude for man nor beast.
When the wind's in the south, of rain there will be fouth.
When the wind's still, no weather's ill.

Buchanan's Almanac—lang foul, lang fair.
What Friday gets it keeps.
Oysters are only in season in those months that are spelled with
    an R.